Crowd Source

Also by

CECILY NICHOLSON

From the Poplars

HARROWINGS

Triage

Wayside Sang

All published by Talonbooks

Crowd Source

POEMS

CECILY NICHOLSON

TALONBOOKS

Talonbooks
9259 Shaughnessy Street, Vancouver, British Columbia, Canada V6P 6R4
talonbooks.com

Talonbooks is located on xʷməθkʷəy̓əm, Sḵwx̱wú7mesh, and səlilwətaɬ Lands.

First printing: 2025

Typeset in Jenson
Printed and bound in Canada on 100% post-consumer recycled paper

Cover illustration via Shutterstock

Talonbooks acknowledges the financial support of the Canada Council for the Arts, the Government of Canada through the Canada Book Fund, and the Province of British Columbia through the British Columbia Arts Council and the Book Publishing Tax Credit.

Library and Archives Canada Cataloguing in Publication

Title: Crowd source : poems / Cecily Nicholson.
Names: Nicholson, Cecily, author.
Identifiers: Canadiana 20240535847 | ISBN 9781772016581 (softcover)
Subjects: LCGFT: Poetry.
Classification: LCC PS8627.I2393 C76 2025 | DDC C811/.6—dc23

for Sandra P. McCauley,
a great reader and friend to the birds

and with love to Brokebeak of Edmonds

And the time in me will hush. And
then we will be listening for real.

—ALEXIS PAULINE GUMBS

Long dark blues
Through the static and distance

—JASON MOLINA

I

those eyes
lined in laughter

fawned
from the floor up

understory
as the
          flies
I hike
carrying my body

to elevation
to rest

a col between
two sisters'
snowy peaks

the alpine air
quality up close

trace elements

ancient
volcanic vents

arched necks
narrow onlookers

behold all colours
in the sun-up
dance
          beautifully

a show of claws *cruaaac-cruaac* slide
sidestep power line

          black brew black brew

too many to be kept off the crop

hollow bones descend
on grain
            sorghum native
forage to Red Sea fields
near ripening corn milk
and dough
            windrowed
peanuts, commercial
sunflowers, pecans
watermelon,
            great game
fruits for many blackbirds
especially grackles

labour
gathered in damage

when the birds visit
country

Arkansas *caw* backstories
brim the lip of silos

adjust with a clattering

they do not scare easily
although they easily scare

forward momentum
clamours

these birds are not dying
they refuse to die

refuse to leave this plane

in fact, existential bullets
shoot out of sockets –
their eyeballs
will not be plucked

that feeling now in my hips
with ruffles

rids the yearning for omens

untuned lately reaching
to grasp at nothing
sound

                    as it once was

whirr, it has been
an accelerated year here

worse and worsening
grasps on situations

a main strategy
is to break

mollusc shells

is to drop them
from enough height
onto the right surface

a neighbouring airfield
other hard tarmacs

a hard practice
                whelk dropping

experiencing the bold
indifference of substrates

urban heat islands
when the winds are weak

traffic against the grain
early for morning

everyday dives bold for carrion
split, gutted, battered

ready for the birds

pulling at the pulp
in the left passing lane
on the Trans-Canada Highway

you swerve to miss them
at great risk

I am grateful

that same drive-by
we were startled again
by a deer plodding
along the median
perhaps searching
            for a way off
the enclosed green strip
partly under construction

its July beams short and spongy
visible from our hurried shell

episodically the call goes out, this poem

writing cars underneath their route
nouns and articles as the day
winds down

working to calm down –
req a dance mix

return to write necessity and detonate

burst iridescence about the barbule
quills of green-bright-trying
ain't no thing but a willing presence

stop in the private tracks of destiny
interrupt its productivity and touristry

the merch is young and fading individuals
more naturally and efficiently into we

towhees, I keep spotting then hearing them

II

soft as fractal
indecision

multiple minds
singular site

cojoined
and occupied

as a bird
sometimes

there are many –
what then

impossible
twilight at the Still

heat distressed holds
on to a low branch
in a stupor

some blackening
medicine needs brewing

yellow leaves breezy
late-afternoon sun dip
behind clouds

hydration –
clogged eavestroughs
the day's rain tea

strength returns in flight
gathering air currents and height

continue in motion or risk running aground again –
for who knows how long

throat movements up and down
rid heat from their bodies

through an open-bill sunbath
terrible heat their throats move

like moulting to extend feather life
this striving is some old way

I learned my old ways on the porch
a worker plus another worker is a crowd

during smoke breaks the loading dock
long ditch walks dusk and night like

fingers fuse to form a rigid platform
form the outer wing feathers

clavicle bones fuse to form a wishbone
increase strength in the shoulder region

flight muscles' place of attachment
rain in the distance is a fair wait still

as this scattering of stars
divests
                from colony
descends
                onto the block
trees, power, and roof lines
early June early evening

shadows speak
in my neighbourhood

the smell of a body lingered
what was still measurable

reconnaissance
on the grounds gathered
a wake assessing for danger

we joined the fray and found seats

taking in a great noise
like nothing we had ever seen

honouring our loss

a montage of heavy rains
run from one big tree to the next

presse

massing together
reasons to gather in purpose

shelter warmth food safety joy
communication
the roots of crowd

positioned as pedagogy
constantly teaching myself
to steady

in the jostling of a throng

for food and foraging areas
information and open images
uncovered domains and subdomains

sharing leverages
vulnerability and exposure
shared knowledge across attack surfaces

open sourcing in a lotic system
perennial streams

outsourced work comes back crowd
broadcasted problems to a public

source aligned in rivulets pushed
through driving wind and rain

in good company
locks rechecked; perimeter alarms set

agitated exchanges winnow
hurried relays
murmur in ascendence
onto lentic rest
the marsh
slow-moving merle dreams

unconscious-wander-with-one-eye-open quality
not your average bug-bounty platform

bring your own unique cultural background
as a member of a global community
best serving the rich
diversity

powering magical experiences
like spotting food or animals in photos
or identifying the emotional impact of sentences

daily solicited from the online open calls
distributing problem solving
in new production models by the hour

litres of water-cooling solutions owned by the entity
who originally broadcast the problem

rewards may include praise or intellectual satisfaction
of volunteer work thriven sparse

analog crowds gather in lessons
learned, queued, ordered
consumption bored (boring)

waiting for the fresh remains
of products
running shoes, doughnuts

ordered crowds line up
two blocks down Water Street
knowing nothing of death
on that street

the beauty
of a crowd marching
in memorial there every year

prayers up, medicine down
the birds know

there even now
in the worst conditions
as new crowds form
gathering more police

amid intensified touristry
who wins the right to be safe
wins sales, property, efficiencies

windthrow rush
events crowd knows
these present holds mark history

provide cover
earmark protests protect
the whirring possibilities

for a golden mile my twenty-five years
of ports and bridges, intersections, libraries
embassies, offices, whose streets
courts, carceral facilities
farms, galleries

crowdfunded barricades resist celebrity

embrace/d in ceremony
winged body black in constellation
feathered muscle over the common

hollow bones are lighter, fly faster
vocal bodies until we disperse
thinking like water
difficult to contain skies and wind

the block we elements shelter soft landings
for hollowed-out heads unhoused in encampments

modular relations refuse
tent city cops for all emergencies

we keep us safe and attend to trial
to soar to persist in how to disperse spells

on a wing's breath
studying for a hex-proof life

sprinting down a crowded avenue
discordant notes bend, we're in a garden

while the blue-black streams above
all songbirds

all songbirds are land birds gathering all this time
how have you been

here all this time on this land and not noticed

III

be slight and showy
matter with gravitas

autumn, slow and dented
closing in

swallows
dodge the nets here

winds have picked up
at a Canadians' home game

meta- and narrative data
overlap out of necessity

innings lean into twilight
fireworks

big lights come on
somewhere cigarette smoke

survivorship
that first year
is about 50 percent

Aggressiveness: 5

What happened: Attacked everyone walking by my home, drew blood in one case. We're all carrying umbrellas now!

DATE: 2023-06-08

we are not easy to communicate with
so often made to be read aloud

interpreters of transcription
too, as black bodies
subject to climate

beaded notes along power lines
at a preroost stop
rapping

musical scores of bodies
become swaps of intel and warmth
with luck, daytime played and nightly rest

where birds rest may harbour
histoplasmosis
fungus harmful to people
who breathe in airborne spores
when soil at a roost site is disturbed

people, do not disturb corvids
at their tavernous hollows
avert your gaze from their torpor
hush as you happen along trails

craaa-aa a raaa in aural lure
assure who is being heard
that you are listening

for birds, animals capable of using
human language inherent
in complex vocal systems
foregrounded calls

quell with small, useful gifts
an unimposing presence, still a threat

tending often to home
to neighbours and neighbourhood

care with blocks of accommodation
a party to

several dozen distinct vocalizations
that when combined with clicks and gestures
                    form the buildings

blocks of complex communication
          demonstrating theory of mind

black as the night is black as their eyes
gather

in neighbourhoods

rhythm and form synthesized *de novo*
inborn magnetite crystals know where to visit

where to flow home to as watershed
gathering numbers across the ethos of east van

quickening messengers flown time immemorial

blooms of soot an everyday Newtonian wash
southern sky at dusk this city late summer

rooks taken flight in a low-end concert theory
of a widely distributed family

the designation of songbirds includes the position
of feet, unconcerned strides like no other

stride street hop lessons well in the anatomy
vocal areas moving as water sheds shores

onto Still Creek independent muscle controls
either side syrinx folds produce different sounds

in theory two different songs that is
two impressive vocal repertoires at the same time

they are large songbirds
with widely distributed family
evolving human speech
in part alarm calls constant
gains of new sounds

loads about the landfill
called murder
throughout their lives
learning alarm calls
great litanies and poetry
great vocal repertoires
for when one dies
and is discovered by another

memorial, a measure of danger
place
          a twig or a piece of grass
     upon a corpse
accumulating coverings
perhaps mount a mating ritual
      or peck and tear
          until no body is left

IV

one some with each other
and one with the world

core unit murmurs

greater than one
entanglement

pair bonds
typically for a life
with dalliances

steady currents
unnoticed throughout

the year tresses on
ribbons of affluencies

elements in common
we are all in and of universe

after

one stretches out its neck

invites allopreening

enduring family
together grooms each other

Aggressiveness: 3

What happened: Group … ate all of my dog's food from a sealed bag, a sealed bag family-sized bag of salt and vinegar chips, a large sealed bag of beet chips.

DATE: 2023-07-30

with episodic-like memory
the caws go out

sharing incidental details
mentally relived

sounds, sights, thoughts
moods at the time

bits of food hidden for later –
a bite of hamburger meat
soaking in the eavestrough

not just knowing –
remembering

embedded topography

how does it feel to be drawn
physically to a place daily

is there a hum to the knowing
a sound or sensation that feels

directional
vocalization with purpose is not a mystical congruity

purposeful vocal control is an aim of communication
speech uses the tongue to count numbers and transmit

articulate quantities classic
american cawww awwwwwwww
northwestern ahhhhhh and all in hybridization

seven caws just now, followed by two crrricks
seven again then two distant, singular notes sound afar
                                        call to take home
four calls issued
from your wavering dips between chimneys along rooflines

go home
                        it's later than you think

        consider this flight path parallel to crisis
scores of blackbirds rally at the port in the north arm
verses away night falls and steams inland

still speaking of value
difficult numerical concepts
such as zero or nothing
are understood as special
quantities

the empty set of a vagabond
to the quantity of family

a mental number line
both behavioural and neuronal
represents an empty set
both creative and practical
rhyme

even when
there are thousands in the sky
the sky is not black with them

the sky is yellowed by smoke

particles irritating airways
fine particulate matter –
nitrogen dioxide, carbon monoxide
and other volatile compounds

destined to sleep in a real place where
thousands objectively are present

feathers formed on primordial scales
armoured hollow bones and bird-brain
materials moulded into flight
          tethered to the stasis of skyline
everywhere horizons sprout

in the saddles of rooftops
an orange sun
                    caught in ribs of cloud

apex anatomy of roof
an owl decoy silhouette

yet, scarecrow tactics won't work
on these dinosaurs

in a matter of days, it becomes clear
the owl remains asleep
no matter the weather, ever perched

The next day, just before dawn, I looked
for them by a car dealership's sign that glowed
over some cottonwoods. A collective lung
... rose in their traffic of hunger.
I inhaled their dry-throated exultation bursting
in all directions. I am alive and ready for the day.

—JEFF STEUDEL

V

forest finds shoreline
a heartbeat

how it streams now
after many lakes

water slowing
refracting
days of light

an eye
to movement

crown and canopy
many snags

clear views
in all directions

soft whistles signal
new entanglements

cultural
followers

everywhere
people live

interact
in pairs

flight posture
and gaze

open, non-pointed – let the bird come to you

young, flew indoors at the airport

people thought to give it a name
Moira, thought to open a twitter account
imagine a bird wit critical of X

Moira, perched
on *Raven Stealing the Beaver Lake*
cedar pole carved by Reg Davidson
at the *Sea to Sky* installation in domestic

a kind of community
Moira, well fed and perched well above
signs asking people not to feed the bird

timely allegory, wayward atop a tree
in its new life

until it's time to return to the flow
via capture and release maybe back to stills
with stories to tell about the inside of a place

interfacing on crowded platform apps travelling light

on the grounds
two of us stop to watch
a campus corvid of the oaks
right a small container still full
of dipping sauce

garbage, all of us
providing so much garbage

invisible until I am seen
in proximation

immediate eyes met
onlooker/looked at

pay us nothing
and go separate ways

nothing familiar yet
in this shared universe
a fiery core registers
as daylight
sun

it's Tuesday morning
hits me straight in the eye

everyone has a story
some have many

studies
stewarding habitat
long-term relations

mishaps and thefts
territorial reckoning

art and mark making

neighbours turned flocks
taken to sky

in highway form

being able to fly is better
than being able to drive

streaming through
dimensions

some ridden by fae
some fae

gathering kith and kin
and messages

mythical beasts herald
the international airport

i. holding a spot
in the parking lot
looking up
endlessly
reaching out
with promise
to a place
that's now here
where you are
now dear

ii. your lunch unattended
food for the birds
top slice of bread hung from a beak
a few instances later you gave up
made acquaintances instead fighting
established reliable patterns
refrained from sudden movements
enjoyed time together
lunching and sunbathing
those last years evergreen

iii. conversation let slip
that the day before
your mother had died
drawing parallels
to found on the floor
and seen in the sky dragon-
two deer peer out fly
from the edge of
a parks' forest
we are visitors
evermore beholden

iv. the last nights
leaning into
the birth
of your first
outside walking
unexpecting
obsidian flows
across the purple
sky promising son
sunrise hastings

v. on your back
in the grass
a tumble
of daughters
about
a sense
still listening as
a hiss of wings
moving air
wishes by

vi. talons clutched
the windowsill
oh my fucking fright
the window
left open that night
a cawing in your face
the room a kafuffle
accursed wakening
yet, you lived to prosper
in love generously

vii. in a valley of vultures
within comprehension
of entrails
endurance gathers
skills to build
and to deconstruct
how to move well with water
good omens after all
like the birds in her hair
and the way silver smokes

viii. where the bridge traffic slips
over stagnant still water
where creek sides are thicketed   you reach
for a red maple leaf
get stung about the ankles by nettle
a good stinging
sometimes it's good to be stung
the pleasant numbing
joints after a long hot day
bumblebees, not a bird in sight

vix. backpack held overhead
suppose I needed
to see this for myself
how the birds in her hair
lift in terror, clammy
uncanny pinches extend
from a rustle the whispers
tether small frays
essayistic black rags
peel back reality hunkered over
in interdimensional ravel

x. empty eyes along an urban corridor
you used to ride your bicycle
jetting downtown for battle against
mechanized old growth media-speak
seeps and spills to kill, capture, take
small nests being damaged, destroyed
removed or disturbed – the small
migratory birds do what they can
drops of water, nest-finding networks
turtles' webbed feet with long claws
semiaquatic futures feel it all, win wars

xi. plays with a small bouncy ball whelk dropping
corner of Moncton St. and Number 1
down the road from historic qʷɬeyəm
in winter
nabs skier's gear from a backpack
stories older than middens at Whyte Lake
white flakes
white blackbird spotted at Bear Creek
Traditional hunting and gathering grounds
wayward genes the brittle feathers

xii. city greenways
underfoot, off-ramp
side streets
no parking or idling
still moon spirit
stream protectors
daylighters, watchers
celebrity admirers
make the news
make possible

xiii. specks yearning
from a balcony
cheers at the buzzer

our pots and pans
red dresses
flags of revolt

resting a moment
in lesser, rented gardens
perched to watch
the moonrise

xiv. hand-raised and exposed
to human objects
Canuck[1] rode the SkyTrain
tried many things
undaunted by humans
this badgering, larcenist, fare-evading thief
was a cultural influencer
resisting criminality and mascotry
gone on five years now
never to be forgotten

VI

indecipherable cause
misunderstood ferocity

common genius
with shadowy purpose

sentinels in a vigil expanse
through a glass, darkly

shadows elongate
the pace of waning light

bell-
wether

hole
in the sky

pattern
frequencies

flap of
two hands

joined at
the thumbs

shadows
static air

lets light
spark

Aggressiveness: 1

What happened: Attacked me out of the blue. For what? it is December, not ... attack season. Weird.

DATE: 2023-12-13

communal roosts
few hundred or millions

some roosts have been forming
in the same general area
for over a hundred years.[2]

short, blunt tail and a strong outline
instantly recognizable

makes for a good shadow in a woodland scene
perhaps observing while the dove and swallow
(easier shadows to move) fly to and fro[3]

late summer to early spring in tributaries
family forms destined for consolidation

sometimes a cloak above Grandview Highway
in parallel commute to the dissociate autos below
(contents possibly alert and moved)

sometimes they fly past my balcony storeys up
could I lean out

we would brush feathers and remember each other
rarely conspicuously alone across open country

rarely flapping in particularly straight lines
maneuvering as the fray demands

wings broad and rounded with the wing tip
feathers spread like fingers

a patient, methodical flapping movement is air
we hear the moving, rare in the city to hear the air

obsidian flyways murder above, talking to the sky, the sky
answers
                    molecular communication flits intricate and
          intimate

auto weight
traffic below bereft, kept in touch   ## has left the march

I am traffic, always looking to the sky   braced for
aggression

confirmed fatalities
slowing to express lanes
                                                            regulated and
                                                  sudden stops

hazy sky the air is filling
more

particles pass through
the palm of my hand
until an asteroid

barely felt specks of fury
and irretrievable loss

are dull thuds
hitting one after another

black-blue constant
streaks of indifference
bedappling street lights
whipping inner space

tonight, the stars, beads
in their open eyes sleep

a bewildering murmur
readying

to do what it takes to keep
respiratory distress at bay

the nature of sources is to attribute citation
sources may form or signify communities
wooded area intermittent creek industrial
high-tech office park poles used for perching
trees: cottonwood, alder, yew, cedar, fir
in a riparian channel harbouring a deep V
inward, to the earth, through to old aquifers

first the waiting-for-kids-to-be-born season
fledglings fight to make flight in the blue
whole as families unlike our voided families
return each night to gather in conference
learning the lay of the land likely close to
four or five before establishing or inheriting
territory the groundwork for co-operative
relations in firm but opaque commitments

having babies and accordant extra vigilance
in the early years the young help
families, as many as fifteen of them
siblings and cousins from different years

juveniles may join gangs of other youngsters
in community after leaving the nest

while family flocks together to the roost
they do not stay together amid the great crowd
valuing collective sun orbit while learning dispersal

find them everywhere

imagine a colloquial entry
to every place in the city

a welcoming is a gift

should one find themselves
present and unscathed
even celebrated

remember that being unwelcome
and hostile is not a crime
and is sometimes necessary

and that an unsafe feeling stemming
from imagined murder, can be killer

just *groups* or *flocks* of birds
were this scientifically family

corridors, sight, ultraviolet light
a view to the hues and patterns
missing from the human
red-green-blue range

ultraviolet as bees see
dark nectar
guides at a flower's throat
auroras of planets, ripe berries
body fluids, bacteria in whitish violet

light on the black tuppence
for the birds, vantablack for all
and for all the creative commons

VII

silver and gold have I none
on the island near here
the most obscure-
seeming owl is nocturnal

bring a light source
and set an aural lure

to realize what's common
pause for the count
and continuity
keep time

blackbirds are common
in the thousands
mythical
about this femme's feet

sun above
silhouettes

harrowing
happenings

a gash
of feathers

pulled from
both sides

ample air in sparse wings

stinging
low tender annual
perennially *th'éxth'ex* stings many times[4]
t'θəχt'θəχ[5]
marshes stream banks with common grasses

Late Pleistocene blackbird
families separated by glaciers
over fossil-rich chalk beds
prior to human settlement
Northwesterners

in the Pacific Northwest
mainly kept to coastlines
beaches and seafood
in particular whelks

back then blackbirds
fashioning beads
onyx of perceptive eyes
abalone primer in feathers
early years alert to arrivals

creek bed a path to a lake in the dry months

water levels are measurable to 15.3 metres
by then has taken the bridges

originating in east van just west of Boundary
behind a playground

an area where it seems the City cares
for wetlands, rain gardens, rainwater
tree trenches flow into a lake created
                    by a glacier
some twelve thousand years ago

please protect our resource
make the gem sparkle again
Lake System Project

put a bird on it

watercourse, fish and wildlife
holdings, freight ways, key investments
yards, dealerships, proposals to enclose

ancient hydrology
used to work perfectly
old-growth forest
full of coniferous trees
slowly filtered
the water down
from the forest canopy
a time when
all of the Pacific salmon
streamed through
Still Creek home
the birds remember
its name, their names

biophobia/philia[6]

culture of social behaviour
generational learning
cognitive sophistication

to evolve within a single generation
via social learning

days foraging
nights in microclimate

a large and singular winter congregation
a relatively recent occurrence

likely the product of different parameters
like large-scale habitat loss, predator protection
and urban food resources

likely endless rivers
move through sky in a welcome unsettling

the hour risen I can hear them just now

It must be emphasized that Still Creek water quality will continue to be subjected to levels of contamination from urban drainage, namely streets, roads, etc. For this reason, Still Creek will not be able to meet public health bacteriological water quality standards for recreational waters.[7]

The Still Creek Streamkeepers are a group of neighbours and citizen scientists who help take care of Still Creek and Renfrew Ravine, with the support of Still Moon Arts Society … This includes water quality testing, ravine cleaning, garbage removal, invertebrate sampling, removing invasive species, and replanting with native plants.[8]

In 2012, chum salmon began to spawn in the Vancouver portion of Still Creek for the first time in nearly eight decades. Salmon spawned behind the Canadian Tire on Grandview Highway in late October/early November five years in a row from 2012 to 2016.[9]

VIII

too
the birds know
more than I can imagine
it is a sweet pastime
to try and to empathize
and to try astral projection
as connections all around
grow colder, more protective
everywhere code switches
you are subject there
involved in the rhythms
with everyday wisdom
looking, I am mainly
listening to know
good to know

INHALE: I deserve more than exhaustion.
EXHALE: I return home to myself.

INHALE: May I rest,
EXHALE: that I may dream.[10]

The conditions just now aligned with all necessary
stars, ancestors in the dark are there in the daytime.

The day-to-day tends to grind and it's hard to regulate
in the nonstop, this vibrating abrading barely contained.

hazing with natural enemies, diurnal raptors such as
red-tailed hawks, cooper's hawks, and peregrine falcons
as they arrive in the later afternoon and early evening

they could be predated upon by nocturnal predators
such as great horned owls, barred owls
as well as tree-climbing mammals like raccoons

once they have settled in for the night

IX

one of the greatest spectacles
the city ever sees

twice daily most seasons
dawn to dusk in lotic spectacle

quantum listening
with an innate sense of numbers

contours sensing a line
between the earth's magnetic field

synthesized *de novo* surviving
billions of years as memories
stored in cells

cells require a storage system
its functions governed by something
quantum
                mechanics extracted here
without understanding

sparkling as receptors in beaks
and nasal passages

embedded in avian living tissue
are wayfinding ways

how metals
magnetize

liquids turn
into gases

systems on
the edge

ready to be
transformed

completely
in an instant

There are two sides to the creek and paths on either side. One is well maintained. Though well-worn, the other is overgrown.

A drive in this lithium-loaded EV sparse on
noise and emissions. An old path, Canada Way
down the hill to the spawning Pacific meets
Central Valley Greenway following contours
and sightlines across municipalities. Avoid
the highway. There is parking at the box stores
institutions, and conglomerate head offices.
Instead I return to a spot used by trucks, an
interstitial stop with no time limits. A wide
gravel shoulder next to a city ditch place to
orient myself. Near the entrance to the roost
there are many dark feathers on the ground
sunken and weathered to rot. They accumulate
more thickly about the sewer drain that's near
the intersection. Far from origins, detached
from epidermal layers, flight feathers separate
from bone and though deadened, are still regal
in this golden light. Some still repel the water.

This visit a walk on the lesser dirt path well used but not maintained. To sit with intention on yesteryear benches by a boxy garbage receptacle that's teeming. Everything grows over everything, the plants now reach over the seat of the bench painted dull reddish-brown blending in. There's a shortcut to the bridge. Evidence of dwelling, spending time eating, fucking, living, and sleeping – smells and refuse. The unnecessary blackberry vines trap the "poor man's" orchid and the morning glory climbs. Leaves of the trees have become scaly. Once ancient woodland: fir, hemlock, cedar, and spruce. A dominant scent reminds me of linden berry. A sweet, seminal rot and slightly off chemical creek, a murky grey-green. Buildings greyish green and the sky this cloudy day refracting composites.

Hear them before they start to arrive. Groups descend over the treetops, surprisingly from behind. Thrilling butterflies, anticipation in the body as the creek draws a crowd. The crowd grows. Thousands were they to turn on me, could whittle me down to the bones. Outward indifference, filling the tops, the lines, wires poles, any structure up high. Each one has their own distinct profile. View from the underside to witness bites out of wings, notches, feathers missing, asymmetrical form. Angles of heads, a range of lengths and widths. Ruffles about the neck, about the crown, and about their feet. Sounds uttered in patterns – occasionally chortles, clicks, and whirrs from a few. Some caws are louder than others, those repeating calls are especially so. Sentinels greeting new groups accompanying them in as they arrive calling out, sometimes turning to look directly as the branching structure starts calling me in.

an intercity path
greenways
upon greenways
small and larger
industry freight
yard and lumber
car dealership
corporate
headquarters
hours bustle in
weekday business
weekend security
mans parking lots
lunch spots
just by the highway
large swishes
roars at all hours
increase in morning
and mid-afternoon
intermittent horns
and various tunings
mainly combustible
engines burning
gasoline or diesel

accompanied and cared for
where were we
                    what was
that highway meets that throughway
or thruway
                    right around the time

the rains begin, early this year (of publication)
point in fact
                    facts, extreme as they are
need feelings, and our intuition ... our intuition is

at the Still, another roost, a rookery isn't quite
right though it's a great word
sentients
back and forth greeting

each new group arriving in twos and tens
security-brief jesters circling, circling

in the little
that was left of the riparian strip[11]

swoops returning to the trees
sometimes the same branch or twig

heavy, shiny, and delicate
in the top branches

how the marshes factor
vegetation strangles
in a sense

the remaining riparian forest
overrun by "Himalayan" blackberry
and "Himalayan" balsam

spread through the watercourses
drought-resistant proliferations
creep the edge of the trail
growing homogeneous stands
of orchid-like blooms in shady sites
intuiting shelter to unhoused homing

the thick monoculture outcompetes
local vegetation along creeks, riverbanks
sloughs, open ditches, grassy clearings

the balsam plant's minimal root system
cannot provide soil stabilization
or protect against high water flows

when the plants completely die off
in winter the ground is left exposed[12]

as autumn closes
our feet crush foliage releasing
a scent like sweet, musty gasoline
glands burst under their leaves

the smell of walking wafts up and out
birds above watching whole times

blackberry perimeters
in some instances
keep bears off a lot
some birds are happy
briar with this dye
and this jelly sunken
benches midday
restful moments
near a rotten bridge
burst of must every
earthbound step lifts
avian notes generally
shifty and expressive

shadows deepen to conceal threats
the blackberries
                  will strangle you
should you weaken
and fall asleep
in the vicinity
                  resting too long
a foot of vine drags your neck
growing slow and painful chokers

thorny ropes let down over skins of alder
branches above banks of wet pink balsam

though the plants retain moisture
and can withstand drought conditions
they are sensitive to frost

pulling the plant by hand
simple and easy

conduct the first pull prior
to and up until the plants flower

before seeds ripen at sites of any size
is the most desirable form of control
          when desirable plants are also present

                    care must be taken
look under vegetation for juvenile plants
along a waterbody
avoid releasing vegetation or sediment into water
avoid disrupting homes or alarming residents[13]

for streamkeepers

dedicated to beauty, living memory
remembers a coal spill, 2015

this geoduck in a sludge
of metallurgical coal

come from open boxcars
come from the Kootenays

topping agents curb coal dust
down the line

spilling into silver light
staccato streams

small little rivers part watershed
            great, great

preservation keeping them well
everyday runs to recover everything

X

blacker berries
a measure of season
gains in sweetness

sieve their seeds out
to make jelly

all the while spreading
being conquered

conscious will invasive
a part of the hue

for the diurnal night
figures shifting

complex pleasure
conspicuously in touch

The birds danced the Sun-Down Dance, then went to nest. All through the night the birds dreamed of black.[14]

They can sleep with one eye open, even while in flight, allowing one side of the brain to rest while the other remains alert.[15]

present in real time
incremental beauty
ricochets

in a bowl of mountains
amid pale blue
twos and tens begin
to ruffle psyches

flutter the hearts of grey
deepening mattes

overhead
edges dissipate
more lights switch on

details dissolve awash
over the corner near
the local bookstore glow
congested shelves
spilling out the door
bathing the street in light

each evening begins earlier

dark earlier
this time of year here
crowds start thinking ahead
to organizing February

managing bodies know it is
the hardest time to get through
and out

ride, walk
it can't rain all the time

in 2020 it snowed
and the alleys
and the sidewalks
and the marching
were icy

with hours of unwanted empathy
weapons to give all at once

in each outlined body, a singular body
is the possibility of collective amassing

tens and tens in the green cast
endless heralding streams

hundreds, thousands

despite ourselves we are caught
looking up for moments suspended
distracted from the everyday routine

familiars above the fray recommitted

despite irretrievable losses
renewal comes in loaming violet hours

The Still

descends into the heart
of its colonial name

night grows dark as it does
and they are

finally, the same colour
as the sky

slightly orange

glinting, even asleep
they are

wind chimes
and weather vanes

feathers freshly molted
ready

for all saints and hallows
heroes ready

for hard temperate rains
and prevailing winds

ocean my lungs exhale
moisture-laden air

masses ready in respire
west coast clefs all the way

steady onto depots
warehouses and institutes

XI

in commute
transit hurtling

through the
Cassiar Tunnel

ready for a
dimensional shift

spatial
and probable

lights slash
the walls open

shadows
rivering out

the corner
of my eyes

headless
horseman feels

tearing home
pursued

at first it seemed they had grown tired on the roof
I found them later the next day in a small garden plot
beside the back door where I used to sit and smoke
            where we had first met a year before

for a while I offer small cups of water, chicken pieces
eventually they lost interest

            light abated our last evening together
petted contour feathers on the crown

my touch caused no outward display of alarm
... slow blinks

            I take the curse
            I stay up late

the next morning   they have left

feathers
not forgotten   remnants

visit and return crowd matter condenses again disperses
again thin forms scatter then strew light about

inky remnants signal in errata
across sky

ragged spots across stave
the call's response

notes slant and blend in relation
rest the night begins to lose its darkness

glowing warm
sound emerges in the blue hours

simultaneous
stirring everyday

hard to say who
starts to move first

and where
along the quiet creek

rustling sound builds
attack and decay

pioneering design
in the misty

morning heart rises
in vortices

black-eyed rising
then dissipating

out to seashores and the landfill

out to the delta containers' port

an old cannery at mock bay

to the playground by the railyard

tinkering farms on the periphery

an earthen dam, a dry creek bed

to an urban lake stocked with trout

or for a guttery bit of brown matter

white-feathered under the wing

atop a wire, looking out on the sea

north shore to the lower mainland

languid busy people landscapes to

swing by and wreck nice lawns after

the beetle larvae loving grass roots

XII

here always
moving

inland
to the riparian

through
the water

under
their sky

never between war or without petty struggles
for existence wills the fiction

attentive to vocabulary and imagery
rather than prosody

now, this problem of prosody ...
and the perception of doing and position

looking or observing changes things, yes

at ball diamonds and
other athletic fields
parking lots, gardens
nearby woodlands
patches of cultivation
beaches, parks, landfills
campgrounds, lawns
cemeteries, playgrounds
on the side of every road
past everyone's balcony
across everyone's backyard

in ascent
not just looking up at the sky
to be *in* the sky powered by
your own body
arms

collective in the expanse
could never just be looking
air, family, feathered, flapping
flight posture in an open gaze

instinctive endowments
anatomically unlike a cortex
for the pallium in clusters

neural interconnections
mediate memory decision-
making cognitive functions
which
              like all of us staring
out at the river
                              watching
water move with endless
variation
                        birds and boats
seals
          suppose
              there is so much more

to see ultraviolet majesty mystery
from the roadside hopping
into traffic to nab food

skirt the rim of dumpsters
casual eaters helping with carrion
after someone else has opened
a carcass to decomposition
to become tender enough to eat

nourishing witness
ruthless in stories of origin
to be intelligence crafting beauty

lotic systems that meander for example
continuously both source and end

constant change winding channels
of erodible alluvial valleys
series of sine-generated curves
and curved flows
alternating banks and shoals
tangled tresses
crowdsourced in murmuration
and other systems

when crystals are formed
avalanche layers deposited by storms
precious bonds vary like all of us staring
in infinite gest as structures replicate glitter

in the dark affinity gathers and offers
feathers and eyes offering gleams
of black receptacles for light

obsidian reflexes a side-eye
to time as it slows to flower

to seed the bare stalk ruddy
resolve into soil

is it better to listen or to talk more
down these corridors of alder
onto a thick, muddy beach
of abalone memory

use your wits

little by little does the trick

necessity is the mother of invention

what is discovered only serves to show
that nothing's known to what is yet to know[16]

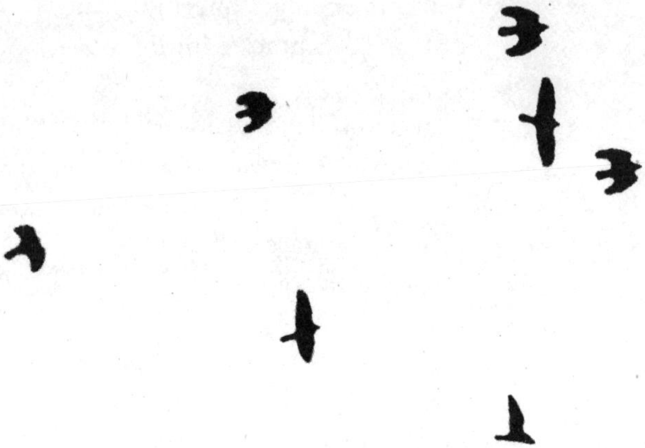

XIII

evening afternoons

snow weight visible in the clouds
too dense for light to shine
through
                    I have a memory
some old path in a park
by the ball diamonds near Fullerton

in winter there under cedar boughs
weighed down in the drifts
was a hovel

I could live there with the birds if needed
                    a hovel away from home

like the poet's blackbird, inured to winter

rest for hollow bones carrying
the weight of feathers
obsidian, abalone, precious metals

wetland warmth subject to expansion
enclosures of marrow and lung

I have cut up a photograph of a falcon and placed in underneath an upside-down wildfire. There is a saguaro in the snow, fragments of a numerical equation.

—AISHA SABATINI SLOAN

I don't know whether the bird you are holding is dead or alive, but what I do know is that it is in your hands. It is in your hands.

—TONI MORRISON

to be still each evening
an intermittent brook there
there is a portal

where gathering crowds led
by silver creek salmonberries
remember the nests

the cups of twigs
lined with softer materials

remember you
as one who was there
in neighbourhoods

neutral ground safety
zones for evacuation

angels or ministries of flight
let them notice your habits
and kindness

your furtive excess open
            to bright disturbances

in a world well past the limit
of my eyesight with its errata

all hope
            grows grit and thick
with these ominous, black specks

Endnotes

1 Bec Crew, "The Misadventures of Canuck, the World's Most Infamous Crow," *Audubon* (website), October 26, 2016, accessed October 30, 2024.

2 "American Crow," *CornellLab All About Birds* (website), accessed October 30, 2024.

3 Sophie Collins, *Shadow Magic: Create 75 Creatures* (Ivy Press, 2021), 104.

4 Stó:lō Elders and Knowledge Keepers and the University of the Fraser Valley, "Th'éxth'ex," *Íhtelstexw Te Shxwelí (Feeding the Soul)* (website), 2022, accessed November 5, 2024.

5 Kalila George-Wilson, "Indigenous Plant Guide: hən̓q̓əmin̓əm̓," *Museum of Vancouver* (website), accessed November 5, 2024.

6 after Christine Thuring, "Crows of Vancouver: The Middle Way Between Biophobia and Biophilia," *The Nature of Cities* (website), April 26, 2019, accessed October 31, 2024.

7 Chief Public Health Inspector, February 9, 1981, "P138 Proposal to enclose portion of Still Creek, 3985 Still Creek Street," City of Burnaby Archives, City Council and Office of the City Clerk Fonds, report ID 1720, item 12.

8 "Still Creek Streamkeepers," *Still Moon Arts Society* (website), accessed October 31, 2024.

9 "Still Creek Streamkeepers."

10 Cole Arthur Riley, *Black Liturgies: Prayers, Poems, and Meditations for Staying Human* (Convergent, 2024), 161.

11 Jeff Steudel, *Foreign Park* (Anvil, 2015), 55.

12 Metro Vancouver and the Invasive Species Council of Metro Vancouver, "Best Management Practices for Himalayan Balsam in the Metro Vancouver Region" (Burnaby, 2021).

13 Metro Vancouver and the Invasive Species Council of Metro Vancouver, 12.

14 Ashley Bryan, *Beautiful Blackbird* (Atheneum Books for Young Readers, 2003), n.p.

15 Candace Savage, *Bird Brains: The Intelligence of Crows, Ravens, Magpies, and Jays* (Greystone, 2018), ix.

16 *Aesop's Fables*.

Further Learning and Inspiration

Rob Butler: robbutler.ca/about

[The] Cornell Lab: www.birds.cornell.edu/home

Crow Attack Tracker: giscourses.net/crowtrax/crowtrax.html

Jake Huang: aristhought.com

June Hunter: urbannature.blog

Still Moon Arts Society: stillmoonarts.ca

Wild Bird Trust of British Columbia: wildbirdtrust.org

Acknowledgments

Poetry is one of my favourite labours. I remind myself as I summon acknowledgments how this work is bound up in gratitude and learning. I wrote a poem about crows over decade ago that arose out of a workshop I took with Marie Clements and Rosemary Georgeson alongside femme community in the downtown eastside of Vancouver. One of the writing exercises centred on a prompt from Marie to complete the phrase, "talking to the sky …" Elegant, immediately we all recalled moments, lying in some itchy grass, wandering down some far-off road, stuck in some nasty situation and peering out the window … looking and inwardly talking to the sky. We summoned poetic prayers. The workshop participants' words were formed into a beautifully mounted theatre performance I'll not forget. I think this book began back then. My inflamed, hypervigilant, fluttering-inside self only is able to focus on poetry for the love of community and with the care of people around me. I hope that love is legible to you.

I finish this book at xučyun, the home territory of the Chochenyo-speaking Ohlone people. Thank you, C.S. Giscombe and folks hosting me as Holloway Lecturer in the Practice of Poetry at UC Berkeley. I am honoured to be a part of this legacy.

Earlier iterations of these poems appeared in a dashing chapbook from Spiral Editions (with thanks to Ryan Skrabalak) – do visit their titles! Work from this collection has also appeared in *The Ear* from Gallery Gachet and as part of the ___*a lineage of transgression*___ exhibition at artspeak, thanks to Nya Lewis and Liz Ikiriko.

Thank you to the team at Talon, I appreciate how much time and resources go into the making and selling of books. I am grateful to Catriona Strang, for your brilliant eye and mediation as an editor. Too, Steve Collis, you've always been able to help illuminate a sensible path through my rambling work.

For bird and habitat consultations, a shout out to my brother Joel (and the spirit of Uncle Roy). To all my family, much love.

Wow, CRWR UBC, thanks for having me. I'm privileged to be in everyone's company and am glad especially, Bronwen, Sheryda, for the notes and readings.

Near and dear, Mercedes Eng, Ivan Drury, Junie Désil, Ontoniya J. Okot Bitek, Hari Alluri, Arlene Bowman, the Lyons and the Kytes, Dallas Hunt, Rita Wong, Nyki Kish, Phanuel Antwi, Dylan Robinson, Suvi Bains, Alanna Edwards, Khari Wendell McClelland, Vanessa Richards, Phinder Dulai, Jeff Derksen, Joanne Leow, Clint Burnham, Emily Fedoruk – dear and far, Neil Brooks (all the Brooks!), Jordan Scott, m. nourbeSe philip, Fred Moten, Juliana Spahr, Tongo Eisen-Martin, Eve Joseph, Patrick Friesen, David Buuck, Christina Battle, Michael Nardone, D.M. Bradford, Jody Chan, and so many workers in the field that I admire, thank you.

Respect and appreciation to those who make the Black Arts Centre and Emma's Acres viable.

To all my familiars … Ru, I wish you could read. Thanks for sitting with me while I've written all of my books. Thank you, Jeffrey. I couldn't be without this joy.

Cecily Nicholson is the author of four previous books, including *From the Poplars*, recipient of the Dorothy Livesay Poetry Prize, and *Wayside Sang*, winner of the Governor General's Literary Award for Poetry. Her collaborative practice spans museum and community-based arts organizing and education. She is an assistant professor at the School of Creative Writing at the University of British Columbia and the 2024/2025 Holloway Lecturer in the Practice of Poetry at the University of California, Berkeley.